COOKING
FOR DORMIES

And Busy People of All Ages

Debbie Jacobson, Ph.D.

BALBOA.
PRESS
A DIVISION OF HAY HOUSE

Author Credits:
B.S. Business Administration and Finance, M.A. Elementary Education, Ph.D. Holistic Nutrition

Balboa Press books may be ordered through booksellers or by contacting:

Balboa Press
A Division of Hay House
1663 Liberty Drive
Bloomington, IN 47403
www.balboapress.com
1 (877) 407-4847

Because of the dynamic nature of the Internet, any web addresses or links contained in this book may have changed since publication and may no longer be valid. The views expressed in this work are solely those of the author and do not necessarily reflect the views of the publisher, and the publisher hereby disclaims any responsibility for them.

The author of this book does not dispense medical advice or prescribe the use of any technique as a form of treatment for physical, emotional, or medical problems without the advice of a physician, either directly or indirectly. The intent of the author is only to offer information of a general nature to help you in your quest for emotional and spiritual well-being. In the event you use any of the information in this book for yourself, which is your constitutional right, the author and the publisher assume no responsibility for your actions.

Any people depicted in stock imagery provided by Thinkstock are models, and such images are being used for illustrative purposes only.
Certain stock imagery © Thinkstock.

Printed in the United States of America.

ISBN: 978-1-4525-1932-6 (sc)
ISBN: 978-1-4525-1933-3 (e)

Balboa Press rev. date: 10/08/2014

Dedication Page

This book is dedicated to every student who considered Ramen Noodles a balanced meal designed for breakfast, lunch and dinner. You can eat better for less than you thought. This cookbook was designed with you and your health in mind.

This book is for you on your journey to your future!

Every food choice you make is either creating
health or disease. You choose!

Acknowledgments

To my husband Eric: you always said you saw my potential. Thank you for loving me, believing in me, and being my #1 fan!

To my chosen family: Linda Sauget, Grace and Jim Barber, Wendy Cerco, Val Jennings, Lynda Hammond, Kelly Beach, Arron Haggart, Steve Bradbery, Terry Conover, Carolina Small, Shantelle Moxie, and AZ. I want to express my gratitude to all of you who continue to inspire me and encircle me with your love. I asked the Universe to send me like-minded people and it responded in a BIG way!

Jamie Oliver has taught me to never stop teaching about how important good nutrition is even though it sometimes feels as though people would rather pay the doctor than the grocer. He makes good food fun and doesn't lecture, although sometimes he does get frustrated. (Me too!)

Thank you to Nadine Gross. I wouldn't be a published book author without her convincing me it was all inside of me and ready to come out and be shared.

Special, heartfelt thanks to my computer guru and mentor, Jim Barber. He always comes to my rescue and certainly understands my frustration with and love for technology in all its forms!

Arron Haggart is my images angel! He was able to convert and resize all the pictures in this book which seemed impossible to me! THANK YOU!

Gracias a la vida que me ha dado tanto!

Contents

How to Use This Book

This book is organized into three parts: Breakfasts and Smoothies, Lunches and Snacks, Dinners and Desserts. I know it is not very original for a cookbook, but when you are tired and stressed, easy is the way to go. I want the book to be easy to use so you will use it!

I have kept the recipes simple and limited to just a few ingredients. The fewer the ingredients the healthier for you and a greater chance that you will actually take care of yourself by cooking nutritious food. I included a Smoothies section in with Breakfasts, however you can make a smoothie any time for a snack or meal replacement. You will find a Snack section in with Lunches, because most likely that's when the need for energy or a craving comes in. No fancy pictures included to make your cooking seem inadequate.

I did not include all the nutritional information for each recipe. If you eat with portion control in mind, and choose good quality ingredients in the first place, you will feel full and be healthy at the same time. I have included dairy products and grains in some but not all of the recipes. There are also choices for vegetarians in here too. This is a healthy cookbook for people on the go who want to use few ingredients and follow simple step by step directions.

I know you want to look good and feel good, but you are on a budget, and stressed for time. What you put into your body is reflected in your skin, hair, nails, and general demeanor. Your brain works at optimum capacity if you feed it well. If you are wiped out, your eyes are dull, your hair is lackluster, and you spend more time trying to figure out how to cover those zits than on researching your term paper. It really is true-you are what you eat.

Remember to look at the list of ingredients before you start to prepare a recipe. It is no fun to start to prepare a meal and then you realize you are missing one or more of the main ingredients. Also, plan ahead. Choose one or two breakfasts, lunches and dinners for the week and jot down ingredients you need on a shopping list. A list will keep you organized and help you stay within your budget.

I hope you enjoy this cookbook and maybe even develop a love for spending time in the kitchen creating delicious and healthy meals. When you prepare your own food, not only do you have the benefit of knowing the exact ingredients, your food automatically becomes infused with love. You were the one who chose each ingredient, cut and/or measured them, and made healthy choices for yourself! When I follow a recipe, I am in the zone! I am focused (wouldn't want to cut or burn myself) and all of my senses are fully engaged. I feel the textures of my food, smell the herbs and spices, and even take a taste now and then to check flavor. I have happy memories from childhood when my home is filled with the aroma of food cooking that I made. What a sense of satisfaction!

I say go for it! Have fun. Experiment with herbs and spices. Try out something new. Make your old favorites. Eating take out, fast food, or frozen make believe meals just can't help you to be the best student possible. Host a study group! Get the family involved. Throw a pot luck feast.

You deserve it!

Breakfasts and Smoothies

Yogurt Parfait

INGREDIENTS:

1 cup yogurt or Greek yogurt if you like
Handful of fresh blueberries and strawberries cut into small pieces
Handful of chopped walnuts
Low fat granola
* Optional: 1 spoonful whipped cream or Cool-Whip

DIRECTIONS:

1. In a tall parfait glass (or any tall cup you have handy in your dorm room), begin to layer all the ingredients. I like to start with spooning some of the yogurt into the bottom.
2. Next sprinkle on berries.
3. Then top with a few walnut pieces and granola.
4. Keep layering until you have used all ingredients.
5. If desired, add a dollop of whipped cream or Cool-Whip on top.

Enjoy! YUM!

BTW- Walnuts look like a brain and are great food for your brain. You can also substitute non-fat plain yogurt to save calories and add Stevia for sweetness. You can use other fruits but berries are loaded with antioxidants and are great for hair & skin. They are also stress fighters.

Health Tip-Go Organic!

Yes, it's true: Eating organic is healthier for you. The fruits and vegetables are grown in healthy soil loaded with nutrients which are transferred to the food you eat. Nutrient dense foods enrich every cell and organ in your body and brain. Here is the dilemma-you are in the produce aisle of your store and you see two heads of lettuce one that is conventionally grown and the other organic. You see right away the higher price for the organic lettuce. So you think about your budget and opt for the conventional lettuce.

Yes, organic produce is more expensive. Organic farmers are held to very strict rules about the quality of their soil, the water conservation practices they use, and organic farmers help to reduce pollution. It is labor intensive and the yield can be less due to crop rotation to keep soils healthy. Most soils are depleted of all nutrients and pesticides are used.

Another consideration is the fact that organic foods don't last as long in the refrigerator. The foods are not treated with preservatives or waxed, so you might have to shop more often. Believe me your liver will thank you for the extra effort.

If a food has the USDA organic label on it, it was produced under highly stringent standards. Organic and "natural" do NOT mean the same thing. All food grown conventionally uses synthetic pesticides to keep insects and mold off their crops. Limiting your exposure to eating these pesticides in your food will protect your health long term.

If you can't afford the organic stuff, locally grown is next best. Local farmers markets are popping up everywhere and offer a great opportunity to be outside on the weekends in the fresh air. Buying this way will have you eating foods that are in season and fresh rather than flown in from another country. It might be nice to eat peaches in winter but fruits imported are treated with more pesticides upon arrival in the United States. You should wash/scrub all fruits and vegetables to remove traces of dirt, chemicals, and bacteria, but most pesticides cannot simply be washed away. Frozen is third and canned is last because of added salt and/or sugar.

Scrambled Eggs with Cheese

INGREDIENTS:

2 eggs, scrambled
1 ounce of cheese, shredded
A dash of milk

Feel free to add any veggies! (Tomatoes can be a bit wet.)

Salt and pepper to taste

DIRECTIONS:

1. Scramble the eggs well in a bowl.
2. Add the cheese and dash of milk to the eggs.
3. Heat the oil, butter or nonstick spray in pan.
4. Pour the egg mixture into the pan and turn down the heat to low so cheese doesn't burn.
5. Keep turning the eggs gently so they cook completely.
6. When cooked, spoon onto a plate. Sprinkle salt and pepper to taste. Have some whole wheat toast on the side with a piece of fruit.

BTW-Eggs have gotten a bad wrap in the press but they are a perfect protein and healthy for you. This meal will fill you and carry you through to lunch.

Cost Saving Tip

Eggs only cost about .22 to .33 cents each for organic and are loaded with important nutrients such as choline (for cognition and mood) and lutein for healthy eyes.

You know you're a college student if ... your idea of feeding the poor is buying Ramen Noodle Soup in bulk.

Hot Oatmeal and Fruit

INGREDIENTS:

1 serving oatmeal
Dash of milk
Cinnamon and /or Stevia to taste

DIRECTIONS:

1. Follow the directions on the box. Please don't buy the instant because it is devoid of all the health benefits of oats. I prefer McCann's Irish Oatmeal. The Quick and Easy Steel Cut takes only 5 minutes to cook.
2. Meanwhile cut up the fresh fruit. You can also buy bags of frozen organic fruit to keep on hand. That eliminates the worry of fruit going bad.
3. Season with cinnamon (which has no sweetness but great flavor) and Stevia with a dash of milk. Stir well. Eat and enjoy with fruit in a cup on the side.

Have you heard about steel cut oats? They take longer to cook, but have a nutty and chewy flavor. I make four servings at a time, and then reheat a serving as needed. Oatmeal is high in soluble fiber, is low in sodium and cholesterol free, and is a low saturated fat. You will feel full and that feeling has staying power.

Peanut Butter-Elvis Style

INGREDIENTS:

2 Tbsp. peanut butter, or almond butter
Sliced bananas
½ tsp. drizzled honey
2 slices whole grain bread, toasted

DIRECTIONS:

1. While bread is toasting, slice the banana. Spread peanut butter on toast. Drizzle on honey, and then top with banana slices.
2. This is fast, easy to eat when you're running late, and so much better than skipping breakfast altogether.
3. The peanut butter (or almond butter which I prefer) is filling and loaded with fiber. If you can buy fresh made peanut butter, do so. The stuff the big brand names have in the jar has added sugar, salt and fat that will slow you down.

BTW- This is a great snack too-a delicious and satisfying energy pick me up.

Overnight Muesli

(pronounced MEYOO-slee)

You can start your day in a healthy way with this recipe because you don't have to cook anything in the morning. At night, when you're awake anyway, mix everything together.

INGREDIENTS:

4 Tsp. old-fashioned oatmeal (not quick-cooking or steel-cut)
1 Tsp. dried fruit
1 Tsp. nuts almonds, walnuts, (sunflower seeds and pumpkin seeds are delicious)
1 Tsp. wheat germ
2 tsp. honey or maple syrup (I prefer agave nectar)
1/8 tsp. salt
¼ tsp. vanilla extract (optional)
A sprinkling of cinnamon (optional)

Choose: either ¼ cup plain yogurt OR ½ cup milk

DIRECTIONS:

Mix all ingredients together in a bowl. Refrigerate overnight.

Breakfast Pizza

Who doesn't like pizza? Breakfast,
lunch or dinner-it's all good!

INGREDIENTS:

1 English muffin or round mini pita bread
2 Tsp. jar tomato sauce
Sprinkles of shredded mozzarella cheese
Any toppings you like: breakfast sausage, pepperoni slices, mushrooms and
spinach

Options: You can even add scrambled or sunny side up eggs and/or bacon
crumbles. You can make it without cheese for a dairy free choice. Also, try
substituting some olive oil instead of tomato sauce if you really want it more
flavored for breakfast.

DIRECTIONS:

1. Put all ingredients on top of the English muffin. Set in toaster oven to
   bake.
2. When cheese is melted and everything sizzling, you are ready to eat.

"When you have something for breakfast, you're not going to be starving by lunch." -Bruce Barton

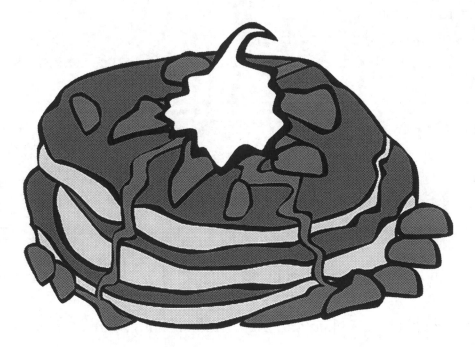

"Not eating breakfast is the worst thing you can do. That's really the take home message." -Bruce Barton

A Few Words about SUGAR

A word about sugar.... People tell me they have heard it is bad for them, but they don't know why. Here it is in simple terms: first of all it is very high in calories, but not filling. You eat sugar, you may have a burst of energy, but then you want more because you crash. Even worse is that sugar suppresses your immune system which is what keeps you healthy and well. Also, sugar creates inflammation, and inflammation is the original cause of all disease. Do you know someone with diabetes? Sugar increases insulin levels. Your poor pancreas can't keep up after a while. Did you know cancer cells *crave* sugar? They feast on it and grow and multiply and grow and multiply.

Stevia, an ingredient used in some of the recipes, is an herb and has been around a really long time. It sure doesn't get the publicity that Splenda (yellow packet), Equal (blue packet) or Sweet N Low (pink packet) receives. The leaves of the Stevia plant taste sweet but have no calories. Some people feel it has an aftertaste and slight licorice flavor.

Don't be fooled by Truvia and PureVia which are highly processed. They take the Stevia and mix it with sugar alcohols. By the time they are done, you would never recognize the natural product.

Another word of warning-sugar is in everything! I mean EVERYTHING! Ketchup-yes! Sugar is even in your salad dressings-especially the fat free kind. Read your labels and you will be surprised. There are over 100 different names for sugar from maltodextrin to sucrose, to fructose and barley malt syrup. The one with the worst reputation is high fructose corn syrup. Do not listen to the corn growers' commercials. It is NOT good for you.

"Give your body the right food
and it will do the right thing."
- T. Colin Campbell

Pizza for Breakfast

We are *not* talking Domino's or Papa John's here! This recipe is good for multiple meals, or multiple people. It is a variation on the Breakfast Pizza on page 11.

INGREDIENTS:

1 small prebaked thin pizza crust

3 eggs

3/4 cups shredded mozzarella cheese

8 bacon strips, crumbled

1 small onion, chopped

¼ cup chopped green pepper

¼ cup chopped red pepper

DIRECTIONS:

1. Place the pizza crust on a greased pizza pan. Use a fork to impress the dough into three equal sections. Scramble the eggs in a bowl.
2. Meanwhile, saute the peppers and onions in butter or olive oil. When the aroma fills the room add the scrambled eggs in a pan. Toss together gently.
3. Put all ingredients on top of the pizza crust, lightly brushed with butter, and bake at 450 degrees F (or follow directions on package) for about 8 minutes.

Each slice is low in calories and the protein will fill you and easily carry you to lunch.

Quickie French Toast

The secret ingredients are the almond butter and jam!
Shhhhh!

INGREDIENTS:

2 slices bread (1 serving)
¼ cup almond butter
¼ cup all fruit jelly or jam
1 egg beaten
¼ cup milk for dipping
Salt to taste
2 Tsp. butter
Confectioner's sugar

DIRECTIONS:

1. Spread the almond butter on one slice of bread, and jelly on the other.
   Put them together to make a sandwich and set aside.
2. Mix together eggs, salt, and milk. Melt the butter in a pan on medium-
   high heat. Dip the sandwiches in the egg mixture, put in pan and brown
   on both sides. Sprinkle with confectioner's sugar and eat immediately.

Yum!

BLT Breakfast Sandwich

with a California Twist

INGREDIENTS:

2 slices whole grain bread, toasted
4 slices cooked bacon
4 tomato slices
2 large lettuce leaves
½ avocado, sliced thinly
Dash of mayo (optional)

DIRECTIONS:

1. Cook the bacon until crispy.
2. Toast the bread.
3. Spread mayo on the toast.
4. Layer on bacon, tomato, lettuce and avocado slices.

What a delicious and healthy way to get the day going, especially when you've got a long day ahead of you without time for lunch.

I'm not sure why California gets credit for using avocado in recipes. Maybe it's because they grow there, but I know they grow in Florida and probably other places too. Hmmm. Anyone know?

Real Vitamin Water

Water is essential for life. I suggest you drink the purest water you can find. If you'd like you can make your own vitamin water and it's easy to do.

Start with fresh water and add desired fruits. You can add herbal tea bags too. Let sit for a half hour. Stir and *drink cold*. No need for sweeteners either.

The store brand of Vitamin Water actually contains approximately 32 grams of sugar. Like electrolyte drinks, all that sugar is not good for you. Think of the packets of sugar you see on a restaurant table. Each one of those packets is one gram of sugar. Can you ever imagine pouring 32 packets of sugar into a drink?

Here are a few ideas:
- fresh cucumber slices
- orange slices
- fresh berries-you can mix it up with strawberries, blueberries, blackberries and/or raspberries
- pineapple and fresh spearmint leaves
- melon water-any kind of melon you like from cantaloupe, honeydew or watermelon

Here is a complete recipe loaded with B Vitamins:
1 slice of lemon
1 peach cut into chunks
5 -6 pieces of pineapple
Handful of raspberries

Place all ingredients in a pitcher with water and leave in the fridge overnight. It is so refreshing and delicious you will be glad you tried it!

Breakfast Tacos

My Texas family *loves* breakfast tacos!

INGREDIENTS:

3 oz. chorizo sausage
4 flour tortillas (6 inch)
3 eggs
Dash milk
½ cup shredded Monterey Jack or Pepper Jack for a kick
¼ cup salsa
Salt and pepper to taste

DIRECTIONS:

1. Crumble the sausage into a pan and heat on medium-high. Cook and stir until evenly browned. Set aside.
2. In a medium bowl whisk together eggs, milk, salt and pepper. Spray pan with Spectrum Organic Cooking Spray and pour in the eggs. Cook and stir until almost firm. Add the sausage. Continue cooking until firm.
3. Warm the tortillas for about 45 seconds per side in another skillet. Make them hot and crispy around the edges.
4. Sprinkle a little shredded cheese on each tortilla while hot and add the egg and sausage mixture. Top with salsa. Roll 'em up and eat!

Breakfast Quesadilla

INGREDIENTS:

2 eggs, well beaten
Sprinkles of shredded pepper jack (or your preference)
2 Flour tortillas- 6 inch
Tomato slices
Avocado slices

1. Pour eggs into a heated buttered pan. (try to use a pan similar in size to your tortillas-it helps with the flipping that comes later)
2. Let eggs cook a bit and sprinkle on some shredded cheese. Place a flour tortilla over the cheese.
3. Carefully place a plate over the egg and tortilla flip it onto plate and then slide it back into the pan, tortilla side down. Let it cook until golden.
4. Add more cheese to the top now. Top with another tortilla and do the plate flip thing again. Let it cook until cheese melts.
5. Slide out of pan. Carefully cut into wedges. Place a tomato and avocado wedge on top. And voila! Delicious quesadilla!

This is another San Antonio favorite!

Easy Pancakes

INGREDIENTS:

1 ½ cups flour
3 tsp. baking powder
1 Tsp. sugar (1 ½packets of Stevia)
½ tsp. salt
½ tsp. vanilla
2 tsp. butter, melted
1 ¼ cup milk
1 egg
Spectrum Organic cooking spray

DIRECTIONS:

1. In a large mixing bowl, combine all dry ingredients. Hollow out a space in the center of the dry ingredients and add milk, melted butter, egg, and vanilla.
2. Use an electric mixer (if not hand mix) on low until all ingredients are mixed well. Scrape sides of the bowl.
3. Spray the griddle with cooking spray. Preheat griddle or pan. Fill a ladle full of batter and pour slowly onto griddle. Repeat-be sure to leave plenty of space between pancakes.
4. When pancakes are filled with small bubbles, gently slide a spatula underneath and flip it. Cook for another 30-45 seconds and use the spatula to lift pancakes off the griddle.
5. Sprinkle with confectioner's sugar, syrup or jelly-your preference.

Green All Your Smoothies

You have probably heard that 90% or more of Americans don't get enough fruits and vegetables in their diets. Are you part of that 90%? Why not try a green smoothie? They are nutritious, delicious, and if you have a blender-a simple way to improve your diet.

Most green smoothies are made up of four things: liquid, fruit, vegetables, and some kind of protein powder. I prefer to use a vegan raw plant based protein powder, but there are many varieties to choose from. Whey powder is used by many, but if you are dairy-free or lactose intolerant this is not for you. (see page 25)

Liquids can be pure water, a milk of your choice (see page 22 for how to choose the right milk for you), or coconut water (my personal favorite). Milks add calories, although unsweetened vanilla almond milk is low (30 calories a cup). Please do not use tap water!

The daily recommendation is to eat 5-7 servings per day of vegetables and fruit. Fruit is high in natural sugar and more caloric than vegetables. Veggies are loaded with protein, yes protein, more calcium than dairy products (milk and cheese), and minerals. Many Americans are deficient in zinc, iron, manganese, magnesium, calcium, and other essential minerals. Eating high quality, organic, vegetables feeds your body what it needs.

You may have heard about other appliances that are better at actually smoothing the smoothie. I agree. I own a Vitamix. Although very expensive, they are built to last. I have mine for years now and it is still going strong. In fact, I always say you could put a rubber tire in a Vitamix and it will turn to liquid!

The saying is true: YOU ARE WHAT YOU EAT!

Choosing the Best Milk
For Your Smoothies

Every smoothie needs some liquid for a base. Water is fine, but has no nutritional value. It also can leave your smoothie a little thin and runny. You can always use juice but remember that adds calories and sugar too. Milk is often used as a base and it does have nutritional value. Milk has protein and potassium. The calcium that the dairy companies advertise is added, (that's what fortified means on the label) and not readily absorbed by the body.

You don't have to use cow's milk. In fact I recommend that you give it up. All species, except humans, drink the milk of their own kind. Maybe that is why so many people are allergic or lactose intolerant, especially babies. If you do decide cow's milk is for you, please buy organic, hormone free and anti-biotic free. What is fed to the cow (anti-biotics and growth hormone) is in the milk which goes into you.

How about almond or coconut milk? Almond milk is a natural calcium and Vitamin E source. Watch for the sugar content if you buy vanilla or chocolate flavors. Almond milk is low in calories and saturated fat, unlike cow's milk which also has to be fortified with vitamin D and Calcium. (Fortified means= added in. They are not found naturally in cow's milk.) Added bonus: no cholesterol or lactose. Coconut milk is rich and creamy. It has a strong and sweet flavor so a little goes a long way. My personal favorite is a combination almond and coconut milk. I don't drink a lot of it, but I do use it in my smoothies.

Other options include rice milk, oat milk, hemp milk, and soy milk. My personal opinion is that no one should be drinking or eating added soy. We have an abundance of it in our food and even in the air. We don't need more and it is linked to breast cancer. As for the others, it is a matter of personal preference.

Apple Cobbler Smoothie

INGREDIENTS:

1/3 cup raw oatmeal
1 scoop vanilla protein powder
1/3 cup chunky applesauce
½ banana (can be frozen)
½ cup milk (see previous page for discussion on milk)
A dash of vanilla
A few shakes of cinnamon
Handful of spinach

Blend until smooth.

Malted Vanilla Smoothie

1 cup milk
½ cup Greek yogurt
1 scoop raw cacao
1 tsp. vanilla
Crushed ice cubes

Blend until smooth.

Pineapple Upside Down Smoothie

INGREDIENTS:

1 cup pineapple, cubed
1 cup milk
½ cup Greek Yogurt
1 banana, sectioned (can be frozen)
¼ tsp. cinnamon, if desired

DIRECTIONS:

Combine banana and ¾ cup pineapple, yogurt and milk and cinnamon. Blend until smooth. Add ice if desired.

Pour over the rest of the pineapple chunks.

Some Protein Powders

Should you add a protein powder to your smoothie? They are an easy to use high-quality protein. They are usually fat and/or cholesterol free and less expensive than meat, eggs or other forms of animal protein.

Whey protein- derived from milk, low fat, great taste, but it is a dairy product and not for the lactose intolerant or allergic, absorbed quickly in the digestive tract

Casein Protein- also derived from milk, absorbed slowly and steadily in the digestive tract, be aware that some people are allergic to casein

Egg White Protein- very low in fat and carbs, cholesterol free, non-dairy (unlike whey and casein proteins)

Vegetable Protein- these include soy and hemp. Hemp is a complete protein and contains all the essential amino acids you need. Also hemp is a low allergen food. Personally I am not a fan of soy at all. It has a strange taste and research is up in the air about its actual benefits.

Brown Rice Protein- least allergenic source of protein, but it is not a complete protein and doesn't contain all the essential amino acids, good for gastrointestinal issues

Flaxseed Powder- not a protein, but high in fiber and contains essential omega fatty acids, also gluten free

Pea Protein- easily digested, gluten free, high amount of protein and amino acids, very soluble, leaves a full feeling longer,

Protein powder can be added to any smoothie to keep you feeling fuller longer. The protein replaces animal sources such as eggs, cheese, and meats.

Strawberry Oatmeal Breakfast Smoothie

INGREDIENTS:

1 cup milk
½ cup rolled oats
1 banana, broken into smaller sections
14 strawberries (can be frozen)
½ tsp. vanilla
1 packet Stevia

DIRECTIONS:

In a blender combine all ingredients until smooth. Add ice if desired. Blend until smooth.

Green Kalie

1 cup almond milk
1 handful organic kale
1 handful of spinach
1 cucumber
1 celery stalk
1 green apple
Fresh squeezed lemon
1 Tbsp. coconut oil

DIRECTIONS:

In your blender combine ingredients until smooth. Add ice.

"Rocky" Smoothie

Green? For breakfast? How about all the Vitamins as in A, C, K, iron, fiber, folate, lutein, magnesium, potassium, protein, and calcium? Not bad, eh?

INGREDIENTS:

1 small banana (can be frozen)
2 cups baby spinach
1 Tbsp. peanut or almond butter (There is also a product called Better n Peanut Butter)
¾ cup milk
½ cup Greek yogurt

DIRECTIONS:

Place all ingredients into blender and blend until smooth. Ice optional, but recommended.

I call this a "Rocky" Smoothie because it is so delicious and filling! It puts a punch into your day when you start it this way! However, if you have blood sugar problems such as diabetes, this is not a good choice for you. Between the banana and almond butter, your sugar will soar. You can scale it down by replacing the banana with a green apple and cut the almond butter in half, or replace it with NuStevia.

Go Green

The green smoothie you can make a meal of...

===

6 INGREDIENTS:

1. Water or milk-hydrates you
2. Fruit-sweet, nutritious, fills you up
3. Greens-energy and power
4. Oats- raw oats, or quinoa (pronounced keen-wah)
5. Seeds or nuts- provides omegas 3 and 6, and protein
6. Healthy sweetener-raisins, coconut, Stevia, agave nectar, dried fruit-pick one

You can always add vanilla extract, herbs like mint, raw cacao, protein powder, etc...

You have everything you need in one drink. Here is the basic recipe, but feel free to experiment.

2 cups water or milk
1 cup oats
2 cups greens (spinach is my preference)
2 bananas
¼ cup dates
¼ cup shelled sunflower seeds

BLEND WELL!

Mean Green Machine

INGREDIENTS:

½ cup blueberries
1 banana
½ cup Greek yogurt
2 cups spinach
1 sweet orange (I prefer navel oranges.)
1 cup of ice
1 cup milk or water

Blend well.

Green Breakfast Smoothie

INGREDIENTS:

Handful of spinach
Handful of strawberries (fresh or frozen)
Handful of kale (broken into smaller pieces, with stems)
½ banana
2 Tsp. almond butter
½ cup Greek yogurt
1 tsp. chia seeds
¼ cup water or milk

This is not very sweet, but has a nutty flavor. Feel free to adjust to your taste preference.

Lunches And Snacks

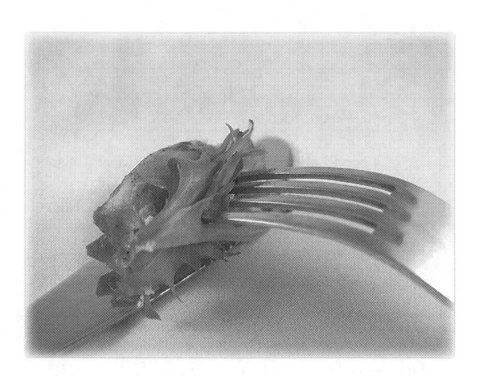

Salads

An Introduction

Salads do not have to be boring. There are so many mixtures of vegetables and fruits, nuts and seeds that you can add. Personally, I prefer NOT to use salad dressings because they are either so loaded with fat or sugar and calories that they take away any health benefit from the salad itself. My personal preference: fresh squeezed lemon and olive oil. You can also use dried herbs and spices such as oregano, basil or garlic powder.

To say I eat a lot of salads is an understatement as at least one of my daily meals consists of raw vegetables in a salad. I love to make sure I change it up all the time for a variety. First of all, variety makes my metabolism keep working at its best. Also, if I get bored I may resort to eating more carbohydrates than I'd like. When you sit down to eat, skip the rolls and dive into a fresh salad.

Eating salads adds fiber to your diet. It works wonders in preventing constipation and has been shown to lower cholesterol levels. You will feel satisfied after having salad as your main meal. You have to do a lot of chewing and since vegetables contain a lot of water you will feel full. Also as long as you stick to olive oil and fresh lemon or vinegar dressing you will be consuming many less calories. Leafy greens are one of the lowest calorie foods. Salad dressing, especially low fat or fat free options contain more sodium and sugar for taste. Try to avoid them! If you add avocado or nuts to your salad you will consume the monounsaturated fats that are good for you!

Salad Makings

A salad is an easy way to eat your veggies. You have probably heard that you need to eat plenty of fruits and vegetables and that Americans aren't eating enough. So how many fruits and veggies should you eat every day? I would recommend you try to eat 5 servings a day, unless you love veggies and then go for more.

I would suggest if you are eating a salad as part of your meal, begin with your salad. It will help fill you up and you will be able to eat more vegetables. It is recommended that half of your plate should contain vegetables, whether raw like a salad, or cooked.

Good news: you cannot make a mistake when you prepare a salad. The health benefits are enormous, just watch out for unwanted extra calories from potato salad, coleslaw, and dressings.

A salad can be very basic: lettuce, tomato and cucumber. Add a little olive oil and fresh lemon or vinegar and you are good to go. But a salad can also be a masterpiece of many colorful and flavorful vegetables.

Be aware that there are many types of lettuce, tomatoes and cucumbers. Walk the produce aisle and check out all the different foods there. See what looks appealing to your eye. Just thinking about it is making my mouth water.

Fixings for a Basic Salad

Lettuce	Tomatoes	Cucs
iceberg	beefsteak	English
arugula	roma	kirby
watercress	cherry	garden
romaine	plum	
red/green leaf	grape	
butter/Boston	ugly	
mesclun/ spring mix		

Lettuce is very low in calories, but loaded with vitamins and phyto-nutrients, folates and minerals like iron, calcium, magnesium, and potassium. It is much healthier to receive these health benefits directly from your food, rather than from supplements. Your body knows what to do with food, how to break it down for maximum health benefit.

Tomatoes are rich in vitamin A, and vitamin C. These vitamins, also called antioxidants, are known to fight off the effects of free-radicals, known to cause cell damage in the body. Vitamin A is known for aiding with improving vision. Tomatoes also contain a high amount of chromium which has been proven to be helpful in controlling your body's blood sugar level. Thus, diabetics will certainly benefit from consuming tomatoes.

The presence of potassium and vitamin B help to lower high cholesterol levels and blood pressure. This will aid in the prevention of heart attacks and strokes.

Tomatoes also have high levels of lycopene which act as an antioxidant, another free-radical fighter.

Cucumbers are a crunchy addition to salads. They are refreshing too. Cucumbers are low in calories and loaded with potassium, and a high amount of vitamin K which helps promote bone strength. Cucumbers are a mild diuretic, and they also make your skin healthier by providing fiber.

Know Your Labels

It is one thing to understand how to read labels on boxes, cans and packages, but it is a different skill set to understand the labels on your produce. Have you ever wondered what those numbers mean on the stickers on fruits and vegetables? You know the ones-the bar code and numbers that appear on produce. Here is what they mean:

5 digit: 9-XXXX
Starting with a 9 is organic

5 digit: 8XXXX
Starting with an 8 is GMO

4 digit: XXXX
Conventionally grown
Contains pesticides

Let me just explain what GMO means as it causes some confusion. The acronym GMO stands for Genetically Modified Organisms. Sounds just like something you want to eat, right? This actually means that the food has been modified, or changed, at the gene level, which means they have been manipulated or altered. New foods, not found in nature, are sitting on grocery shelves waiting to be purchased. In 1996, the first large-scale commercial harvest of genetically engineered crops increased. If you purchase foods that contain soybeans, corn (including high fructose corn syrup, soy flour, corn oil, corn starch, soy isolates, and/or soy oil) you are consuming GMOs.

Right now the laws do not mandate that GMO foods be labeled, many organic producers are labeling their products as GMO-Free.

<u>Here are a few rules I use in the produce aisle</u>:

1. Buy organic.
2. Buy locally grown fruits and vegetables.
3. Buy what is in season.

List of Salad Vegetables

You can add any vegetables that you like. If you like it, you will eat it. Here is a partial list of possibilities:

Beets
Broccoli
Green onions-also known as scallions
Radishes
Cauliflower
Mushrooms
Carrots
Jicama
Shredded cabbage
Diced sun dried tomatoes
Peppers- green, yellow, orange, red
Zucchini
Squash
Asparagus
Celery
Edamame
Peas
Radicchio
Artichoke hearts
Spinach
Bok Choy
Sprouts

Red Bermuda Onion
Cherry Tomatoes
Avocado

<u>Herbs add flavor</u>: basil, oregano, lemon pepper, parsley, cilantro, rosemary, tarragon, mint

Don't forget to add nuts! Almonds, walnuts, pumpkin seeds and sunflower seeds add flavor and fiber. They are healthy fats for your body and brain. Remember-your brain is made of fats and water. Feed it!

Caprese Salad

INGREDIENTS:

Arugula
2 sliced tomatoes
2 oz. mozzarella thinly sliced
5 thin slices sweet red onion, optional
Kalamata olives, optional
1 T olive oil
balsamic vinegar
fresh or dried basil

DIRECTIONS:

1. Slice the tomatoes and cheese thinly.
2. Place arugula on a plate.
3. Layer cheese, then tomato, then basil.
4. Drizzle olive oil and balsamic vinegar over the top.

Options: add some crusty garlic ciabatta bread, Kalamata, green or black olives for more color and flavor!

Caprese Salad Skewers

<u>This is a variation on the previous recipe.</u>

1. On medium length skewers - a cherry tomato, a round mozzarella ball, and a basil leaf. You can also use green olives or kalamata olives.
2. Place on a tray and drizzle with olive oil, basil, oregano and white balsamic vinegar.
3. Easy to prepare and great for a party.

My local grocery store sells three different length wooden skewers: short, medium and long. You can also find them in the kitchen gadget section of many stores.

Couscous Salad
(pronounced Koose-Koose)

INGREDIENTS:

1 pkg. whole wheat couscous
1 can artichoke hearts, quartered, drained
1 bunch fresh spinach, chopped
1 can Garbanzo beans, wash and drain well (also known as chickpeas)
4 oz. Feta cheese
Kalamata or black olives, sliced
½ fresh squeezed lemon
Olive oil

DIRECTIONS:

1. Follow directions on the box of couscous. I like to use Near East brand because it takes minutes from stove to plate.
2. Meanwhile wash and drain artichoke hearts and garbanzo beans. Wash the spinach and chop it.
3. Slice the feta and olives.
4. Put all ingredients in a bowl and mix.

This is a delicious and filling meal. It is so easy to make and travels well so it is great on the go!

Health benefits of couscous:
- Low in calories (fewer than rice or quinoa)
- Good source of protein
- Fiber- lowers cholesterol and helps in weight loss
- Loaded with essential vitamins like thiamin, niacin, riboflavin, B6, folate and pantothenic acid

Farfalle Pasta Salad

(bow tie shaped pasta)

INGREDIENTS:

1 lb. piccolini (means tiny in Italian) farfalle pasta (also known as bow ties)
Black olives
Strips of sun dried tomatoes
Fresh cherry tomatoes, broccoli florets, & red pepper chunks (feel free to add any other veggies you like)
4 oz. Mozzarella or feta cheese-cut in chunks
Olive oil & balsamic vinegar
Toss, chill & eat
(variations: add peas, beans, etc...)

DIRECTIONS:

1. Cook pasta according to directions. Let it cool a bit.
2. Add other ingredients.
3. Mix well. Keep refrigerated.

Greek Garbanzo Bean Salad

INGREDIENTS:

1 can garbanzo beans
1 cuc, halved lengthwise and chopped
6 cherry tomatoes halved
½ red onion, chopped (onion always optional)
2 minced cloves of garlic (also optional)
1 can black olives, drained & chopped
2 oz. crumbled feta
½ lemon, squeezed,
olive oil to taste
salt and pepper to taste

Combine all ingredients. Toss. Refrigerate 2 hours before serving. Eat with pita bread or naan.

JOKE:

What do penguins love to eat?

ICEBERG lettuce! (get it?)

Greek Lentil Salad

INGREDIENTS:

½ cup lentils, cooked according to directions
¼ cup each: chopped tomatoes, chopped cucumber, chopped red onion
2 T red wine vinegar,
1 T olive oil
¼ cup feta
2 t oregano

Combine all ingredients. Toss well. Keep refrigerated. Eat with pita bread or naan.

Lentils are very healthy!

- They are associated with lowering cholesterol because of the high fiber levels.
- Many Americans are deficient in magnesium which can be difficult to absorb taken as a supplement.
- Lentils are high in magnesium and folate which improve blood flow and oxygen and nutrients throughout your body.
- Fiber is great for good digestive health in preventing constipation. Fiber and the complex carbohydrates in lentils increase your energy level because they are slow burning.

Linda's Bow Tie Pasta Salad

INGREDIENTS:

Tri colored bow tie pasta
Red pepper, onion, mushrooms, spinach, garlic, fresh tomatoes, sundried tomatoes
Enrico's traditional pasta sauce (1/2 packet of Stevia added)
Shredded parmesan cheese

DIRECTIONS:

1. Cook pasta according to directions on the box.
2. Saute the veggies in a pan with olive oil. (Saute means to fry quickly in hot oil.)
3. Combine pasta and veggies with pasta sauce and sprinkle with parmesan cheese.
4. Bake at 350 F just to warm it all up and melt cheese.
5. You can eat this hot or cold. Refrigerate leftovers for the next day.

My friend Linda likes to keep her recipes simple. Just a few ingredients go long on flavor! The tri-colors make it as much fun as Linda is!

Summer Couscous Salad

INGREDIENTS:

1 can chickpeas, washed and drained
1 cucumber, diced,
1 orange bell pepper, diced
1 zucchini
1 yellow squash
raw sunflower seeds-a few handfuls
1 cup (before cooking) couscous
Seasonings-salt, pepper, garlic powder, oregano, basil

DIRECTIONS:

1. Cook couscous to directions.
2. Cut the zucchini and squash into slices. Saute gently in olive oil until softened.
3. Add all other ingredients. Toss. Refrigerate.

This is very light and flavorful.

Couscous-
- Provides essential nutrients for your overall health
- Good source of non-animal protein
- High in fiber
- Contains thiamin, niacin, riboflavin, B6, folate and pantothenic acid-in other words excellent for skin, blood, brain, nervous system, heart, and immune system!

Sandwiches

Sandwiches are an American tradition. They are compact, easy to make, travel well when you are on the go, easy to eat, no mess, and no clean up. There are sandwiches and then there are sandwiches. They can be boring if you don't liven things up a bit. The recipes I include here are not your everyday cold cut sandwiches. You don't need a cookbook for that.

Just think Dagwood Bumstead!

(If you never heard of Dagwood, he is an old comic strip character from *"Blondie"*. He is famous for his tall, no better to say skyscraper tall multi-layered sandwiches loaded with breads, meats and cheeses, and a variety of condiments.)

Hummus, Olive, & Tomato

INGREDIENTS:

Hummus as a spread
Whole wheat English Muffin
Sliced tomato
Green olives, or olives of your choice, sliced
An orange

DIRECTIONS:

1. Toast the English muffin.
2. Spread with hummus.
3. Top with sliced olives and tomato.
4. Eat the orange at your next break.

Hummus: (pronounced Hum-us)
- A dip made of chickpeas (garbanzo beans), olive oil, lemon juice and salt with many different varieties available
- Rich in non-animal protein
- Associated with lowering cholesterol and weight loss
- Balances blood sugar
- Some studies say it can reduce your risk for cancer
- Part of the "Mediterranean Diet"

Simple recipe to make your own hummus:
In a food processor, add 1 can chickpeas washed thoroughly, a garlic clove, extra virgin olive oil, lemon juice and salt.

Not an Ordinary Grilled Chicken Sandwich

INGREDIENTS:

Grilled, baked, or roasted chicken breasts
Crusty bread
Tomato slices
Avocado slices
Bacon slices
Lettuce

DIRECTIONS:

1. Prepare the chicken breasts by washing and drying them. In a bowl mix together salt, pepper, garlic powder and some olive oil. Mix into a paste and brush on chicken. Grill, bake or roast the chicken breasts.
2. Meanwhile cook the bacon and drain the fat. Slice the tomatoes and avocado.
3. You can put dressing, mayo or mustard on the bread according to your preference. Put the chicken on the bread. I prefer to slice the chicken into strips because it is easier to bite into without making a mess.
4. Add the tomato, avocado and bacon.

Bacon Guacamole Grilled Cheese

INGREDIENTS:

4 strips of bacon, cooked
1 ½ cup shredded Monterey Jack cheese
1 avocado
½ fresh lemon
1 roll or sourdough bread

DIRECTIONS:

1. Make the guacamole by peeling and mashing the avocado. Squeeze on the fresh lemon. Mix well. Set aside.
2. Cook the bacon well. Drain.
3. Get the pan hot. Butter the bread. Put half the cheese on it followed by the bacon and guacamole. Put the rest of the cheese followed by the other half of bread-butter side up.
4. Cook until bread is crisp. Carefully flip to cook other side.
5. Spread the guacamole on both sides of the bread.

This can be messy but oh so worth it!

Grilled Portobello/Burger Sliders

INGREDIENTS:

Small hamburgers
Portobello mushrooms
Slider rolls
Sliced red onion
Sliced cheese, your preference
Sliced tomato
Garlic powder, olive oil
Ketchup, if desired

DIRECTIONS:

1. Broil the burgers in the oven, or cook in a pan on the stove to desired wellness.
2. Brush the portobello mushrooms with garlic powder and olive oil. Grill for about 3 minutes. Brush the other side and flip. Grill until softened about 3 more minutes.
3. Lightly grill the onion slices until softened and slightly browned. Toast the slider rolls.
4. Put sliders together. Top with cheese and tomato slices, grilled onions and mushrooms.

Eggplant-Red Pepper Melt

INGREDIENTS:

1 eggplant
1 red pepper
4 oz. mozzarella cheese
Olive oil
Crusty bread-French or Italian or even ciabatta

DIRECTIONS:

1. Slice eggplant and brush with olive oil. Slice red pepper in half. Place on top of eggplant skin side up.
2. Broil 4 minutes. Turn eggplant, not red pepper. Broil another 4 minutes.
3. Broil red pepper additional 7 minutes until blackened.
4. Melt mozzarella on top.
5. Put on a crusty bread. For more flavor make the bread garlic bread by spreading with melted butter and garlic powder.

Eat immediately. SOOOOOOOOOOOO delicious.

So What Is Protein Anyway?

Protein is an essential nutrient for all ages. Protein can be in combination with fat as in animal protein, or seeds and nuts. Protein can also be in combination with carbohydrate, as in beans and grains. Lentils are loaded with iron and protein. Garbanzo beans (also called chickpeas), black beans and kidney beans have lots of protein as well. Protein powders have become very popular for shakes and smoothies. Be wary and read labels. Look for sugars that are high in carbohydrates. This can undo all the healthy goodness of a smoothie. For example, I love Whole Food's Kalicious! Mmm! Then one day I asked and almost keeled over when I was told each smoothie has 36 grams of sugar! No wonder it tasted so darn good!

Before I go further I need to say I do not include soy here because I do not believe it is healthy for anyone. (Maybe that's why it is used so much in highly processed foods?) Studies prove it is loaded with estrogen, and we already have enough of that. Also, it is linked to a slow thyroid. Soy is linked with interfering with mineral absorption too. If I see by reading the label a product has soy in it, I put it right back. Soymilk for infants has also been studied and found to be unhealthy.

Protein does not only come from animals. Animal protein should be lean and includes: duck, chicken, beef, pork, venison, fish, and shellfish. Eggs are a lean protein. Beans, seeds and nuts count as protein and so do vegetables. Surprised? High counts are found in: avocado, broccoli, spinach, peas, artichoke, asparagus, and beet greens. Quinoa (pronounced KEEN-wah), brown rice, buckwheat, and barley are protein-rich foods.

By the way, other studies have been done linking protein at breakfast with the ability to sleep well at night by producing melatonin and serotonin. Try to avoid cereal for breakfast and have some protein. See if it helps with your sleep.

Wraps

Wraps are often made with tortillas. They are the perfect size and shape to stuff, fold and eat. Pita bread and Naan bread works too. Other things you can try are lettuce leaves, spring roll wrappers (wanton wrappers) or crepes.

Wraps provide variety which alleviates boredom and they are handy. You put everything in, roll it up, pack it to go, and it's still all nice and ready to eat when you are. I love to make a wrap filled with leftovers. I have created some tasty meals that way.

Try some different kinds of sauces too. Don't overdo it, or your wrap will fall apart and you will add untold calories.

How to wrap:
- Lay out your tortilla, naan or pita bread on a flat surface.
- Line up the ingredients in the center and don't go too close to the ends.
- Fold about three inches of each end in toward the middle.
- Then roll the rest of the tortilla around the fillings.
- Make it snug. Then slice in half on a diagonal.

Crunchy Veggie Wrap

(My personal favorite!)

INGREDIENTS:

1 cucumber, sliced thin
1 chopped tomato
2 slices onion, I prefer red onion
Handful of sprouts
Handful of shredded red cabbage
A few crumbles of feta cheese
Pita bread, tortilla, or Naan
Ranch or dressing of your choice

DIRECTIONS:

1. Cut the pita bread in half.
2. Fill half of ingredients on each side.
3. Drizzle the dressing on top.
4. Wrap and pack to go.

Options:
Feel free to experiment with different breads, different veggies and different dressings. Sometimes I just use whatever leftovers are in the fridge that wouldn't be enough for a meal on their own. Many wraps use cream cheese instead of dressing. Feel free to try that too.

Chili Tuna Pinwheels

INGREDIENTS:

6 oz. tuna, drained
2/3 T sweet chili sauce
A handful of chopped green onion (also known as scallions)
2 flour tortillas
Cream cheese

DIRECTIONS:

1. Mix and blend tuna, chili sauce and green onions in a bowl. Blend in a bit of water to allow easy spreading.
2. Spread a thin layer of cream cheese on each tortilla and cover the entire surface.
3. Spread the tuna mixture over the tortilla to within an inch of the edge.
4. Wrap them up.

Options:
These can be refrigerated or frozen until you are ready to eat them. Just wrap in aluminum foil. Give them 15 minutes from the freezer to defrost.

When ready to serve, you can cut them into small slices about 2 inches each. I call them pinwheels.

BLT Wrap

INGREDIENTS:

4 Slices cooked bacon
2 flour tortillas
½ cup shredded cheddar cheese
Lettuce leaves
Tomato slices

DIRECTIONS:

1. Cook the bacon until crisp. Drain. Set aside.
2. Sprinkle the tortillas with the cheddar cheese. Melt in a pan or microwave.
3. Immediately top with bacon, lettuce, and tomato.
4. Fold up the tortilla and wrap it snugly.

Options:
You can use mayo rather than melted cheese.

The debate- turkey bacon VS pork bacon:

There is a raging debate that pork bacon is fattier and higher in calories. I would suggest READ THE LABELS! As far as calories go, the difference is slight. But reading the labels may show turkey bacon with some strange ingredients. Rule of thumb-if you can't read it, don't eat it! Check sodium levels too, not just calories. Read the small fine print at the bottom and then choose what you think is best for you.

Chicken Salad Wrap

INGREDIENTS:

4 oz. chicken, cooked and shredded or diced
Some chopped onion
Diced tomato
Mayonnaise, to spread on 2 tortillas (another alternative is ½ mayo, ½ mustard)
Lettuce leaves
Salt and pepper to taste

DIRECTIONS

1. In a small bowl combine the chicken, onion, mayonnaise, salsa and salt and pepper if desired. Mix well.
2. Place lettuce leaves on tortillas. Divide the salad mixture into two equal parts. Place on tortillas.
3. Wrap them up.

Options:
You can use leftover chicken or canned chicken. If using canned, drain well, and flake with a fork. You can also try Dijonnaise. It tastes great-nice silky and creamy texture, with mayo at 90 calories a serving and Dijonnaise only at 53.

Greek Pita Wrap

INGREDIENTS:

3 oz. cooked chicken, shredded
Handful of chickpeas (garbanzo beans)
Handful of crumbled feta cheese
Mayonnaise
Lettuce leaves
Chopped tomato
Chopped onion
Dried oregano
Squeeze of fresh lemon
Dash of garlic powder
Pita bread, cut in half

DIRECTIONS:

1. In a medium bowl mix mayonnaise, a squeeze of fresh lemon, beans, and garlic powder. Mix well.
2. Stir in remaining ingredients except for lettuce leaves.
3. Cut pita in half. Fill with chicken mixture.

Options:
You can leave out the chicken and just have the beans. Also you can exchange hummus for the mayonnaise.

Spanish Rice Wrap

INGREDIENTS:

½ green pepper, chopped
2 celery sticks, chopped
½ red onion, chopped
2 cups cooked long grain brown rice
½ tomato, chopped
2 flour tortillas
Sprinkle of Monterey Jack cheese

DIRECTIONS:

1. In a bowl combine the green pepper, celery, onion, and cooked rice and mix gently. Add the tomatoes. Mix well.
2. Place the filling on the tortillas and sprinkle with the cheese.
3. Refrigerate before serving.

Afternoon Snacks

Snacking

People have a snack in the afternoon for different reasons. Some do so to curb overeating later on. Avoiding getting too hungry is a good idea for most of us. Other people need a small snack to keep their energy levels high.

Too many people reach for a candy bar or other sugar filled treat. While in the short run you might feel energized, then you will crash. You will crave more sugar and so the cycle begins.

Having some carbs at lunch and then following up with some protein for a snack will keep your energy level, and keep you from the sleepy slump. You will stay full longer and prevent over-snacking.

Snacking is not necessary. If you are eating well balanced meals three times a day, that should suffice. Only Americans seem to snack between meals, and we are among the most obese in the world. Often referred to as SAD, the Standard American Diet is made up of highly processed foods, tons of sugary donuts-cookies-brownies-candies, high in simple carbohydrates and low in fruits and vegetables.

Starbucks and a muffin or to change things up a donut and Dunkin' coffee for breakfast, grab a quick pizza special from one of the chains or a sub sandwich, and dinner is bring in take-out or restaurant dining. Fast food is the norm in American society. Then we wonder why we are stressed and exhausted but meanwhile we haven't fed our bodies or brains.

Many times, we aren't actually hungry, we are thirsty. Did you know that by the time you feel thirsty, you are already dehydrated? If you want to test your actual hunger vs thirst, drink a glass of water. Wait a few minutes and see if you feel satisfied.

Never get too hungry, angry, lonely or tired!

Edamame

(pronounced Ed-uh-mom-ay)

Organic edamame make a delicious snack. I buy them frozen and take out a serving as needed. I let them thaw. Then I add a dash of coarse sea salt. You can buy them in the pod or loose. I prefer them in the pod because it is a bit of work so it takes more time to eat them. They are low in calories, have fiber and protein, contain iron, Vitamin A and calcium. They do have healthy fats too.

Chickpea Nibbles

When you roast chickpeas in the oven, they become a crunchy snack.

INGREDIENTS:

1 can chickpeas, washed and drained
1 T extra virgin olive oil
Dash garlic powder
Dash crushed red pepper-this is spicy-use sparingly until you are used to it
Dash salt and pepper

DIRECTIONS:

1. Preheat the oven to 450F.
2. Dry the chickpeas with a paper towel. Mix all other ingredients in a bowl.
3. Add the chickpeas to coat well.
4. Spread on a baking sheet.
5. Place in the oven about 30 minutes until the chickpeas are brown and crunchy.

Hard Boiled Eggs Stuffed with Guacamole

INGREDIENTS:

2 eggs
1 avocado
Salt and pepper
Fresh squeezed lemon

DIRECTIONS:

1. Cook the eggs in boiling water for 20 minutes. Drain. Let them cool. Peel. Set aside.
2. Make the guacamole by peeling the avocado and mashing it in a bowl. Squeeze in fresh lemon, add salt and pepper. Mix well.
3. Cut each egg in half. Add the yokes, if desired, to the mixture. Mix well.
4. Spoon the mixture into the egg halves.

Options: I have seen guacamole that has chopped tomatoes and onions as well.

Trail Mix

I like to make a lot of this at one time. Then I put single servings in snack size baggies. When I'm busy, I can grab a baggie and go out knowing I have a healthy snack with me.

I prefer to use raw nuts and seeds. The more the nuts are roasted and salted the less healthy they are. They do not have as much flavor, so I will usually choose one item that is roasted and salted to add to the trail mix.

NOTE: I did not include peanuts because so many people are allergic to them. If you do not have a problem, you can add them.

INGREDIENTS:

Raw almond slivers
Raw cashews
Raw walnuts
Dried apricots
Dried cranberries
Roasted and salted sunflower seeds
Roasted and salted pumpkin seeds
Chocolate chips or raw cacao nibs

Blend all ingredients together in a large bowl. I make a lot so I make it once and then divide it into smaller single portions in baggies.

Fruit and Almond Butter

INGREDIENTS:

An apple or banana
Almond butter

DIRECTIONS:

1. Spread almond butter on apple or banana slices.

Hummus with Veggies

INGREDIENTS:

Hummus
Fresh veggies: baby carrots, cucumber slices, celery sticks, red pepper slices,
Broccoli and/or cauliflower florets

DIRECTIONS:

1. Dip the vegetables in the hummus.

Options:
Baba Ganoush and taboule are alternatives to hummus. Try something new!

Rye Crisps with Avocado

INGREDIENTS:

4 Rye Crisps
A dab of hummus on each
4 slices of avocado

DIRECTIONS:

1. Spread a dollop of hummus on each rye crisp and add a slice of avocado.

Options:
Add a dollop of cream cheese or a half slice of cheese on each crisp instead of hummus.

Crumpets with Honey

INGREDIENTS:

1 crumpet
A drizzle of honey

DIRECTIONS:

1. Warm the crumpet.
2. Drizzle honey on top.

Options:
An English muffin toasted.

Eat Half

Save half of each meal. Eat half your breakfast and take the other half to go. Eat that about 2 hours later. Then at lunchtime, eat half your sandwich or wrap. For your afternoon snack, eat the other half. At dinnertime, eat half. Around 7:00 p.m. eat the rest. Try to avoid eating anything too heavy at night. Those calories will stay with you forever.

Sunflower Seeds
A Special Nut

Eating seeds from their shells takes longer and helps you consume fewer calories as you work to remove the seed from the shell. They are portable and you can grab a handful on the go. Carry them in your purse, car or backpack so you will always have something to pick at.

Dinners

What Makes A Balanced Meal?

Let's keep this really basic. I don't believe it is healthy to eliminate any food group from your diet. It is very difficult to maintain long term, and your body needs a variety of foods from every group to maintain health. A balanced diet provides your body with enough nutrients for proper function and nutrition. However, people with chronic diseases may need to adjust their diet. Every one of us is very individual in our needs and a professional should be consulted if necessary.

The basic groups are: grains, vegetables and fruits, protein and fats. I like to include water as a food group. It is the most important fluid you can consume. Eating from all the food groups, rather than eliminating certain foods completely, is the best way to eat a balanced meal.

I would suggest starting your dinner meal with a salad. An alternative would be looking at your plate and filling about one third of it with vegetables. Another third can be lean protein or a protein alternative. The last third should be from the grains group which includes rice, potatoes, bread and pasta.

Think color when making a choice from any food group. The darker the color, the more nutrient dense the food is. Choose red grapes over white grapes. Pick a sweet potato over a white potato. Brown rice is healthier than white rice. Dark grainy breads have more nutrients than white bread, etc...

Zucchini Sticks

INGREDIENTS:

2 zucchini, halved
9 cherry tomatoes, halved
Extra Virgin Olive Oil
Garlic Powder
Salt and Pepper to taste
Shredded Parmesan cheese

DIRECTIONS:

1. Preheat the oven to 375F.
2. Grease a baking pan and lay out the zucchini halves.
3. Brush with olive oil.
4. Sprinkle with garlic powder, salt and pepper.
5. Place three halved cherry tomatoes on top of the zucchini halves.
6. Bake until soft, 20-30 minutes.
7. Sprinkle Parmesan cheese on top of zucchini sticks until melted.

Options:
You can use any vegetables you like. I have made the same recipe with eggplant and red peppers. You can also make this into a sub by putting it on toasted Italian bread.

Chicken Parmigiana

The chicken in this recipe can be fried; however you will save extra calories if you bake it instead. I love this recipe because it is quick to put together and the oven does most of the work.

INGREDIENTS:

2 boneless chicken breasts
1 egg
¼ cup milk
Italian seasoned bread crumbs
Extra virgin olive oil
4 slices mozzarella cheese
Jar of spaghetti sauce
Parmesan cheese

DIRECTIONS:

1. Preheat the oven to 375F.
2. Whisk the egg and milk together in a bowl. Dip the chicken in the mixture and then in the bread crumbs.
3. Place the chicken breasts in a lightly greased baking dish (use the olive oil). Pour some spaghetti sauce on top.
4. Bake until chicken is tender probably 40-45 minutes.
5. For the last 5 minutes, put the mozzarella cheese on top to melt.

To balance the meal, I suggest starting with salad and garlic bread. You can also make a side dish of spinach or broccoli.

Debbie's Quickie Italian Spaghetti Sauce

INGREDIENTS:

1 can diced tomatoes
1 can crushed tomatoes
1 onion, chopped
2 garlic cloves, minced
Extra virgin olive oil
Oregano, basil, garlic powder, salt and pepper to taste

DIRECTIONS:

1. Heat the oil in a pan on medium-high heat. Add the onion and garlic and toss them until fragrant.
2. Fill the crushed tomato can with pure water and add in small amounts to desired thickness.
3. Add the spices.
4. Cover and simmer for 20 minutes.

I know, I know. You can go buy a jar of sauce for a couple of bucks and save some time. But there is an art to cooking your own food; knowing every ingredient that goes into the pot, lovingly preparing each one, and a great sense of satisfaction when you sit down to a healthy meal made by your own two hands. No artificial colors, flavors, or preservatives-just whole, natural foods.

This is my own sauce. It is a marinara sauce with lots of taste. My mother-in-law didn't use onions in her sauce and she used tomato paste. My own mother does use onions and crushed tomatoes. So I took the best of the two different recipes and created my own!

Can't you just smell it simmering?

Spaghetti and Meat Sauce

INGREDIENTS:

½ pound lean ground beef or turkey
1 onion, chopped
2 garlic cloves, minced
Spaghetti sauce
Whole wheat pasta
Extra virgin olive oil
Parmesan cheese

DIRECTIONS:

1. Heat oil in a pan on medium high heat. When hot add onion and garlic. Toss in the oil until fragrant.
2. Add the meat and stir until brown. Adjust the heat as necessary.
3. Meanwhile boil water in a pot for the spaghetti. Cook according to the package directions.
4. Add the spaghetti sauce to the meat mixture.
5. When the spaghetti is done, drain.
6. Place on plate and ladle sauce mixture on top. Sprinkle with parmesan cheese.

To make a balanced meal, start with a salad and garlic bread. Another option would be to start with celery sticks, carrot sticks, broccoli and cauliflower florets with Italian dressing for a dip.

Chicken Cacciatore

INGREDIENTS:

1 pound chicken, cut into pieces
1 onion, chopped
2 garlic cloves, minced
1 green bell pepper, chopped
1 can diced tomatoes
1 cup fresh mushrooms, quartered
1 can sliced black olives (optional)
Garlic powder, oregano, basil, salt and pepper to taste
Extra virgin olive oil
Linguine

DIRECTIONS:

1. Heat oil in a large pan on medium-high heat. Add the chicken pieces turning to prevent sticking. Remove the chicken and set aside.
2. Add the onion, garlic and green pepper to the pan until the onion is browned.
3. Return chicken to the pan and add the tomatoes, and spices. Cover and simmer for 30 minutes.
4. Meanwhile boil water and cook the linguine according to the directions on the box. Drain when done.
5. Add the mushrooms and salt and pepper to taste. Simmer 10 more minutes.

This is a complete meal with lean protein, vegetables and grains.

"Healthy" Fats?

Contrary to many fad diets out there, fats are good for you and actually *needed* by your body to be healthy. It is necessary to understand the difference between healthy and unhealthy fats. Udo Erasmus wrote *Fats That Heal, Fats That Kill.* This book was required reading for my doctoral degree in nutrition.

As you can probably guess, fast foods, fried foods, and hydrogenated oils are the No-No fats. But did you also know to include vegetable oil, pasteurized dairy and powdered eggs? Yes sir. These are No-No fats too. Oils that are odorless and colorless are not good for you.

The healthy fats include:
   *First cold press, extra virgin olive oil (it will say that on the label)
   *Organic chicken and eggs
   *Avocado
   *Raw nuts and seeds (great snack foods)
   *Grass fed beef (look up CFO's for more graphic info on regular beef)
   *Raw organic coconut oil (which is also great for hair and skin)

Fats, the healthy ones that is, make up about 50% of our cell membranes. Since you have approximately 60 TRILLION cells in your body that would be significant! The fats help add to strengthen the membranes and add rigidity. Healthy fats help get the calcium into your bones because it is converted into Vitamin D. To support your immune system, healthy fats create a healthy intestinal lining to protect against autoimmune diseases.

Personally, I do not support any "diet" that asks you to eliminate one or more of the food groups. Your body was built to require all of them: carbohydrates, fats, protein, and pure healthy water. (You do not need to eat dairy to have strong bones. The Dairy Association has done wonders to convince people of that.) It is a matter of eating cleanly-pure, organic, whole foods is what creates health!

Easy Baked Ziti

INGREDIENTS:

1 box of ziti
1 container ricotta cheese
1 (4) cup package shredded mozzarella cheese
16 oz. Debbie's Quickie Pasta Sauce or 1 large jar prepared sauce

DIRECTIONS:

1. Preheat the oven to 350F.
2. Cook the ziti according to package directions.
3. Spray with nonstick cooking spray a large casserole dish. Set aside.
4. Drain ziti and place in a large mixing bowl.
5. Mix in the full container of ricotta cheese.
6. Mix in half of the shredded mozzarella.
7. Mix in half the spaghetti sauce.
8. Put sauce on the bottom of the casserole dish.
9. Pour the ziti mixture into the dish. Pour on the rest of the sauce.
10. Layer with the rest of the shredded mozzarella.
11. Bake about 20-30 minutes until the cheese is golden and bubbly.

Burger Sliders

INGREDIENTS:

1 lb. ground beef or turkey
1 egg, scrambled
3 T bread crumbs
1 package slider rolls
Lettuce, tomato, onions

DIRECTIONS:

1. Scramble the egg and mix with the ground meat and bread crumbs in a bowl.
2. Form small burgers by rolling the meat in your hands and then flattening.
3. You can bake them in the oven at 350F or cook on top of the stove in a pan. Cook to your preference of wellness.
4. Place burgers on slider buns, top with lettuce, tomato slices and raw or sautéed onion.

Options:
You can top with cheese or guacamole. You can add a side of cole slaw or potato salad too.

Chicken and Broccoli Stir Fry

INGREDIENTS:

2 chicken breasts, cut in strips
1 onion, chopped
2 cloves of garlic, minced
Bean sprouts, snow peas (optional)
Fresh broccoli florets
Teriyaki sauce
Extra Virgin Olive Oil

DIRECTIONS:

1. You can marinate the chicken in teriyaki sauce for a few hours, or even overnight, for added flavor.
2. Heat oil in pan, add the onion and garlic. Quickly stir in the chicken so it cooks on all sides. Add the broccoli florets. Keep tossing. Add the teriyaki sauce. If you have bean sprouts add those too.

You can serve this over fried rice.

Fried rice recipe:
Make rice the day before. Heat a small amount of oil in a pan. Scramble an egg and add it to the rice with some soy sauce, peas and carrots. Cook until well mixed and hot.

Eggplant and Pepperoni Sauce with Pasta

INGREDIENTS:

1 onion, chopped
2 cloves garlic, minced
1 eggplant, cut into 1 inch hunks
1 stick or package pepperoni
1 can crushed tomatoes
1 can diced tomatoes
Extra virgin olive oil

DIRECTIONS:

1. Slice onion, garlic and eggplant.
2. Saute the onions and garlic in olive oil.
3. Add the cans of diced tomatoes and crushed tomatoes. Add one can of water. Mix well.
4. Add the eggplant. Allow to cook on low heat for about 20 minutes. The eggplant will cook down and get smaller.
5. Add the pepperoni. Allow sauce to simmer gently for an additional 30 minutes.
6. Taste it. Add garlic powder, oregano, salt and pepper to taste.
7. Cook pasta of your choice according to directions on the box. Drain well.
8. Ladle sauce on top of pasta.

I originally tasted a similar sauce in "New Corner Restaurant" in Brooklyn, N.Y. I took the flavors that I tasted and went home and created this recipe.

Why Use A Slow Cooker?

1. There is just one pot to put everything into and just that one same pot to clean up.

2. You can throw in anything you have left over and it cooks well. Vegetables that have started to wilt go well in a slow cooker. You can also use cheaper cuts of meat.

3. Your room/apartment/house will smell delicious. You will have fond memories of a home cooked meal when you use a slow cooker due to the fabulous smell that permeates the whole place.

4. Slowly cooked food is tender and full of flavor.

5. What could be more convenient than throwing everything into a pot and leaving for the day?

6. I have never heard once of a slow cooker dish that didn't work out. So, be assured you can't make a mistake. It's foolproof!

Pot Roast with Veggies

This recipe creates a delicious home cooked meal like Mom, or Grandma, used to make. It is tender, juicy and comforting.

INGREDIENTS:

1 small roast beef (about 2-4 pounds)
1 package brown gravy mix
4 carrots
2 stalks of celery
An onion, chopped
2 garlic cloves
8-10 new potatoes (small red potatoes)
½ cup of water

DIRECTIONS:

1. Place roast beef in pot.
2. Sprinkle brown gravy mix over the top.
3. Wash and cut vegetables. Place in pot.
4. Pour in the water.
5. Cover and cook on low about 5-6 hours.

Dig in! Slow Cooker Chicken

INGREDIENTS:

1 roasting chicken, cut up
1 onion
1 package fajita mix

DIRECTIONS:

1. Stuff the peeled onion into the chicken cavity. Remember to wash the chicken and remove giblets from inside the cavity.
2. Place the chicken pieces into the slow cooker.
3. Sprinkle the fajita mix onto the chicken. No water is needed. The chicken makes its own juices.
4. If you want to add any vegetables, cut them and add them at this time.
5. Cook on low 4-6 hours.

Barbecue Sweet Meatballs

This one is super easy!

INGREDIENTS:

1 (32 oz.) bag frozen ready-made meatballs
1 (9 oz.) jar of grape jelly
1 (18 oz.) bottle of spicy barbecue sauce

DIRECTIONS:

1. Combine the jelly and barbecue sauce in the slow cooker.
2. Then add the meat.
3. Cook on high for 2-21/2 hours until completely cooked through.

You can always make your own meatballs:
1 lb. ground chopped meat
1 egg
4 T Italian seasoned bread crumbs.

1. Mix all ingredients in a bowl. Mix well.
2. Make meatballs by rolling a small portion of meat between your hands.
3. Place in slow cooker with the jelly and barbecue sauce.
4. Follow slow cooker directions above.

Slow Cooker Lasagna

INGREDIENTS:

½ lb. ground beef

1 diced onion

1 garlic clove, minced

12 oz. spaghetti sauce

½ cup water

1 (8 oz.) container ricotta cheese

1 cups mozzarella cheese

¼ cup Paremsan cheese

1 whole egg

6 uncooked lasagna noodles

DIRECTIONS:

1. Brown the beef and onion and garlic in a saucepan.
2. Add the spaghetti sauce and water. Simmer for 5 minutes.
3. In a bowl, mix the ricotta, half the mozzarella, half the parmesan cheese and egg.
4. Pour about 1 cup of the meat sauce into the slow cooker. Place half the noodles and half the cheese mixture on top of the sauce. You can break the noodles to make them fit. Cover with more meat sauce. Top with remaining noodles and cheese mixture.
5. Add any of the other ingredients leftover.
6. Cook on low 4 hours or so until noodles are soft.

Note: Do not try to speed up the process by cooking on high. It doesn't work.

Desserts

Here is my disclaimer-the small, fine print

These recipes are
Delicious
Fattening
Loaded with sugar
Use processed foods

But taste yummy!

Chocolate Pretzel Treats

INGREDIENTS:

20 small mini pretzels
20 small Rolo chocolate candies
20 pecan halves

DIRECTIONS:

1. Preheat oven to 300F.
2. Arrange pretzels in a single layer on a parchment lined cookie sheet.
3. Bake for 4 minutes. When the candy is warm, press a pecan half onto each pretzel.
4. Cool completely. Store in an airtight container.

Options: You can use different kinds of candies including caramels. You can use walnuts instead of pecans as well.

Angel Food Pineapple Cake

This will satisfy any sweet tooth, is quick and easy to make, and low in calories.

INGREDIENTS:

1 Angel Food Cake Mix
1 can unsweetened chopped pineapple
1 container Cool Whip (optional)
Fresh strawberries or blueberries (optional)

DIRECTIONS:

1. Empty contents of the cake mix into a bowl. Add the pineapple. Mix well.
2. No other ingredients necessary. Even though the recipe on the back of the cake box tells you to add other ingredients, don't.
3. Follow the baking instructions on the package.
4. Cool. Add Cool Whip and fresh berries if desired.

Ice Cream Sundae

INGREDIENTS:

Ice cream flavor of your choice
Chocolate or caramel syrup
Sprinkles
Cookie pieces
Banana sliced in half
Whipped cream
2 maraschino cherries

DIRECTIONS:

1. Slice a banana in half and place in dish.
2. Add scoops of ice cream.
3. Pour on toppings. Add sprinkles and cookies pieces.
4. Top with whipped cream and cherries.

Indoor S'mores

INGREDIENTS:

Bag of flat large marshmallows
Graham crackers
Chocolate bars pieces
Chocolate sauce

DIRECTIONS:

1. Preheat oven to 300F.
2. Set up a single layer of graham crackers. Place one chocolate square and a marshmallow on top of each graham cracker.
3. Cook for about 5 minutes until marshmallow and chocolate soften and melt.
4. While still warm drizzle chocolate sauce on top.

If you can't use heat at all-substitute fluff for marshmallows and Nutella for the chocolate bars. Just spread on the graham crackers and yum!

Fruit Pie

If you haven't tried this yet,
you are missing a delicious treat!

INGREDIENTS:

1 pie crust (ready to eat)
1 (8oz) package of cream cheese
2 T milk
¼ cup powdered sugar
2-3 cups assorted cut up fruit

DIRECTIONS:

1. Preheat oven to 450F. If raw, bake 9-11 minutes until browned. Cool completely.
2. In a small bowl beat cream cheese, milk, and powdered sugar until smooth.
3. Spread pie crust with cream cheese mixture. Arrange fruit on top. Chill in refrigerator until ready to serve.

Dessert Nachos

INGREDIENTS:

½ cup sugar

2 t ground cinnamon

1 refrigerated pie crust, softened according to directions

1/3 cup hot fudge sundae syrup

1/3 cup caramel sundae syrup

½ cup chopped nuts

DIRECTIONS:

1. Preheat oven to 350F. Spray a cookie sheet with non- stick spray.
2. In a sandwich size plastic baggie mix sugar and cinnamon.
3. Unroll the pie crust onto a cutting board. Cut into 3 inch wide strips-cut strips into triangles that look like nacho chips.
4. Add a few triangles at a time to the bag with sugar cinnamon mixture. Toss them to coat them well.
5. Place in single layer on cookie sheet. Bake 10-12 minutes until golden brown and slightly crisp.
6. In two separate bowls, heat the sundae syrups on high for 5-10 seconds until warm enough to drizzle.
7. Immediately remove pie crusts from cookie sheet and drizzle with chocolate fudge and caramel sundae syrups.

Options include: marshmallows, chocolate chips, coconut flakes, and fruit.

Many nutritionists and health experts talk about the Standard American Diet (SAD). It is also referred to as the Western Diet. How many of these can you identify with?

The typical American....

Eats fast food at least 2 times per week
Eats out an average of 4-5 times a week
Shops at malls at least once a week
Drinks 3 cups of coffee a day
Drinks 2 carbonated beverages per day
Takes prescription drugs
Is overweight
Eats a donut or muffin for breakfast
Rarely eats dinner as a family
Rushes through a meal
Uses a cell phone during meals-may even sleep with one
Has diabetes
Eats at their desk at work
Buys brand name products
Is easily influenced by advertisements
Lives vicariously through celebrity lives/"reality" TV
Has a high school education
Suffers from at least one addiction
Eats white sugar, white flour products
Eats more packaged food than fresh food
Eats in their car

My challenge to you is to see how many of these habits you can knock out of your life and start living healthier and happier! Go for it!

Works Cited

By Chernface141 (Own work) [CC-BY-SA-3.0 (http://creativecommons.org/licenses/by-sa/3.0)], via Wikimedia Commons http://commons.wikimedia.org/wiki/File:BuscemiHeart.jpg

"Coturnix coturnix eggs". Photo by Mnolf. icensed under Creative Commons Attribution-Share Alike 3.0 via Wikimedia Commons - http://commons.wikimedia.org/wiki/File:Coturnix_coturnix_eggs.jpg#mediaviewer/ File:Coturnix_coturnix_eggs.jpg**http://en.wikipedia.org/wiki/Egg_(food)**

http://www.publicdomainpictures.net/view-image.php?i mage=42780&picture=grapefruit-and-cherry

http://www.publicdomainpictures.net/view-image. php?image=4051&picture=bowl-of-ramon-noodles

http://commons.wikimedia.org/wiki/File:Bw.jpg

http://www.clker.com/clipart-72189.html

http://www.publicdomainpictures.net/view-image.php?image=608&picture=lunch

http://www.publicdomainpictures.net/view-image. php?image=43140&picture=green-salad-and-tomatoes

"Dagwood" by EncycloPetey - Own work. Licensed under Creative Commons Attribution-Share Alike 3.0 via Wikimedia Commons - http://commons.wikimedia.org/wiki/File:Dagwood.JPG#mediaviewer/File:Dagwood.JPG http://en.wikipedia.org/wiki/Dagwood_sandwich#mediaviewer/File:Dagwood.JPG>

http://commons.wikimedia.org/wiki/File:Sunflowers_seeds.jpg

http://www.publicdomainpictures.net/view-image.
php?image=30624&picture=fork-spoon-amp-knife-set

http://www.publicdomainpictures.net/view-image.
php?image=44561&picture=balanced-meal

http://www.publicdomainpictures.net/view-image.php?image=85865&picture=red-pot

http://www.publicdomainpictures.net/view-image.php?image=610&picture=chocolate

Index

About the Author

Debbie Jacobson is a native New Yorker who has lived in El Salvador, Guatemala, Mexico, Arizona and Florida but has somehow managed to keep the Brooklyn accent with slightly nasal undertones. Her Spanish accent is pretty darn good. One of her favorite pastimes is seeing the look on people's faces when she begins a fluent conversation in Spanish.

Blessed with a most understanding and supportive husband, Eric, she lives in Tamarac, Florida. Bella, an 8 pound rescue Yorkie-Poo also runs the household. Our daughter Barbara and granddaughters Xoe and Xamara light up my life. Becoming a member of The Grandma Club changed my priorities completely-now we have fun!

Interestingly, Debbie has a B.S. in Business Administration, and an M.A. in Education and has been teaching 28 years, so far. She decided to go for a doctorate in Holistic Nutrition and received her Ph.D. in December, 2009. She has studied the Emotional Freedom Technique, the Neuro Emotional Technique, Nambudripad's Allergy Elimination Technique, and Reiki with certification I and II.

Debbie is working with clients to help them transform their lives, considering herself to be the guide on the side as she educates, motivates, and inspires others on their journey of healing body, mind, and spirit. You can check out her web site:

www.debbiejacobsonphd.com

Her personal journey has been long and full
of lessons. And it ain't over yet!